LOVE'S RED DOOR

*Renewing your community
with a respite park*

by
Allegra Jordan

To everything there is a season, and a time to every purpose under the heaven... A time to weep, and a time to laugh; a time to mourn, and a time to dance...A time to love, and a time to hate; a time of war, and a time of peace.

–Ecclesiastes 3:1;4; 8

CONTENTS

May You Have Joy

It's all right to flourish, to smile and to have joy, even today.

There is much wrong with the world. This is true. And there is also love and laughter. If we forget that love, fun and laughter also exist, and that suffering does eventually cease, we become cynical and make worse decisions for ourselves and our community.

If we are going to interrupt the current cycle of violence in which we find ourselves, we need to bring our best mind, body and spirit to our community. We also need to learn from our greatest failures, wounds, and scars. In these wounds, we find great insight. There we find the antibodies that create healing medicine for the world.

In the following essays, I invite you to learn about what a respite park does through an extended example of Rick's Place in Fayetteville, North Carolina.

A respite park helps you have fun and be seen by your community. A respite park lets you run around, read books, tell jokes and act silly in wholesome ways. It feeds you a modest meal and listens to what you like to do so some time in the future the group activity can attend to your delight.

At this free 50-acre outdoor park, we do just that. Service members and their families come for organized fun, free activities and a free meal once or twice a month. Examples include water-games, rustic competitions, horse rides, gardening and once a year, the visionary set architect behind the American Ninja Warrior sets creates stunning Vegas-style obstacle courses (over water) for families. The park is open every day, dawn-to-dusk with books in free libraries and sports equipment available (pending COVID-19 restriction permission). In summer, kids can come to a fee-based day camp (SFQ-Camp or Super Fun Quality Camp) which is generously underwritten by the local minor league baseball team.

What can a respite park do? That is up to the individuals who enjoy them. Individuals are the agents of their own growth.

Here is one letter from a soldier who helped Rick's Place from its earliest days. He and his family volunteered for the past five years, and his job took him to a new post.

In December 2019, he wrote,

"Since the beginning of Rick's Place, my family and I have volunteered and taken part in various events, and invited numerous people to come out and enjoy one of the many family-friendly events Rick's Place hosted.

I remember my oldest son and I going to the monthly work events and working from around 0800 till about 1400. I never would have imagined the skills I would develop by volunteering. Skills like being a team leader and becoming more vocal.

I became a better leader by working in small groups and sometimes on projects of my own. I remember taking charge of numerous tasks like chopping trees and clearing out fields, or as they call it here, lawnmower therapy. One of my greatest challenges was for me to take charge. I have always been good at listening and following directions, but when I was put in charge I was forced to become more vocal and make decisions to help us get the job done right and on time.

Looking back over the years, I feel a sense of gratitude from what transpired from a field covered with trees containing a trailer, an old tractor, and an old stable. I am grateful because Rick's Place and its facilities helped me grow out of my shell to become a better husband, leader, and follower of God.

Thank you for all you have given me."

Very respectfully,
[Name withheld]

I first came into contact with the idea of a respite community when I worked at the University of Texas at Austin, from 2000-2006. One of the great anti-domestic violence leaders in our country, Professor Sarah Buel, asked me to help her replicate the Relief Nurseries of Oregon on behalf of Texas' social services.

"Relief nurseries are proven to be one of the top ways to stop domestic violence and child abuse because they prevent the harm from happening in the first place. A potentially violent parent get supports and de-stresses before he or she hurts anyone," she said.

I read the copious research which showed that when a community creates a loving and supportive space, good things can happen and bad things can get worked out before the problem can becomes catastrophic. I signed on and provided modest volunteer help in its early stages before my family moved from Austin to North Carolina in 2008.

In North Carolina, I brought the idea of a respite park but found no takers. What I did find was the global reconciliation movement and the hospice movements. Work in these movements helped set the foundation for my work with military families, the case study I describe in the following essays.

When I started working with military families around 2016, I had not set foot on a military base in almost forty years. I had no close military friends. My father had died a few years before of complications from Agent Orange poisoning from the Vietnam War.

I did have memories. My first memories in life were from life in Manila, Philippines at Clark Air Force Base in the early 1970s. I especially loved chewing on sugar cane or visiting the Jungle Survival zoo (of sorts).

Some of my happiest memories were at McGuire Air Force Base in the mid-1970s, when the US Air Force was not the place you wanted your beloved parent to be. But life on base can be fun for military children. As a lot, we are curious and energetic, loving to ride down the street on our bikes or climb the monkey bars at a local playground. On base, I could easily round up five to ten kids on my street to play with.

Yes, in service, our parents could die at any moment, but if we were on base, then it had not happened yet. (The truth is that any of us could die today, we just walk around like we won't.) For much of my young life, my father was stressed by his job, but my father also liked his job until the end of his career when the US Air Force took dubious actions to contract its force. My father was a pilot who transported supplies in C-141s. He would later tell me the best times of his work life were when he flew at night over a mountain range, between peaks and clouds and a luminescent moon.

I knew my father was being targeted by his command, but I was shocked when my family actually left McGuire.

My father woke me up before dawn that June morning in 1977. My dad, no longer Major Malcolm E. Jordan, as he was now out of service, carried me, a skinny, 8-year old, pajama-clad, brown-hair, blue-eyed kid, to our waiting car which had the engine running. He tucked me in back bench of our lime green Ford LTD alongside my two brothers. My baby sister was nursing in the front seat with my mom. Before the sun rose that day, we left the McGuire Air Force Base and the US military where he'd honorably served for seventeen years.

I never went back. But as many people in the military now, even if you went back, your community has disappeared. There is nothing to return to.

Many years later I had language to describe my father's journey with the military: it was one hell of a hard knock. The Buddhist call it the worldly winds: joy and sorrow, praise and blame, gain and loss, success and failure, pleasure and pain. They're all there for everyone. Not just him. Not just me. And we each respond to deep disappointment differently. It's a mystery who some have more resilience than others. The wound was deep for my family and in that wound I learned quite a lot.

My family moved to Selma, Alabama where my father had bought a house during his pilot training. I was now in hot, rural Alabama and I had a New Jersey accent. This was a painful experience for me. I was lonely. In a few years of our arriving, the base closed, our house burned down, and my father's hardware store shuttered in the first wave of "big box store" expansion. On the upside, I poured myself into studies and the town supported a champion debate program which helped me get a college scholarship. I also saw up close what happens in a town after the Civil Rights victory parades are over.

During this time of uncertainty, golden memories from my childhood on the military base became a critical asset for my survival. When I would feel lonely and defeated in my new town, I would conjure them back up in my mind's eye. I would smile thinking of playing with friends in a field. The thrill of riding my chopper-style bicycle with its white wicker flower basket between the handlebars down the street as fast I could. I delighted in the time I got to take a picnic lunch with my best second grade friend to 'Clay Canyon,' a hill on no known map except the one etched in my heart. We rolled down sideways over and over again until we were clay covered.

Those moments helped me know what "right" felt like. I knew what it meant to be loved and held in someone's heart on those days when I felt so lonely. Those golden moments some days were not only my salvation – but my hope.

Great Russian novelist Fyodor Dostoevsky wrote,

"You must know that there is nothing higher and stronger and more wholesome and good for life in the future than some good memory, especially a memory of childhood, of home. People talk to you a great deal about your education, but some good, sacred memory, preserved from childhood, is perhaps the best education. If a man carries many such memories with him into life, he is safe to the end of his days, and if one has only one good memory left in one's heart, even that may sometime be the means of saving us."[1]

In 2016 my husband, who teaches ethics at Duke University, taught an ethics workshop to soldiers. One soldier approached him after with a plan for a respite park that he and others had been creating, the plan that became my full-time job from 2017-2020. The soldier described a park where military families could re-bond in-between deployments. The park had a made a good start, attracting volunteers and a handful of critical financial supporters. But the team had a big idea of having the park replicated at every military base where service members were heavily deployed.

I was invited to sit in on Board meetings. I eventually was asked to serve on the volunteer Board and, the next year, to serve as executive director.

From 2016-2020, I drove more than 80,000 miles between my home in Chapel Hill, North Carolina and Ft. Bragg, the largest military installation by population in the world. It was a four-hour, $30-a-tank round trip that I'd do two to four times a week, and I'd do it with joy. I could help kids feel loved, just like a handful of adults helped me feel loved so many years ago when I was on base.

The mission of "Rick's Place" was to help a community of service members and their families build a free park dedicated to helping military families re-bond in-between deployments. The real story, however, was to build a place where love was in abundance.

Today the foundation, the Rick Herrema Foundation, is a platinum-rated 501(c)3 non-profit. It was founded in 2014 by friends and family of the late SFC Richard J. Herrema who was killed in action in 2006 during Operation Iraqi Freedom.

The foundation's mission is to strengthen relationships and to build community for the Military Family through fun, quality activities. RHF's pilot park is called Rick's Place, a 50-acre park is located 5.5 miles from Ft. Bragg, the US' military's largest installation by population.

To enter the Rick's Place welcome center, you must pass through a red door with a Gold Star affixed to it. When I became executive director, I'd inherited a house that could use a fresh coat of paint. I bought a bright red can of Benjamin Moore paint and got to work. I found a rustic star at Hobby Lobby and spray painted it gold. (Later the luxury bronze sculptor Marc Cervarich of Sun Valley Bronze made a custom Gold Star knocker in bronze.)

It's a fact that a person died before we had eyes to see the pain that constant deployments were causing. It took much pain to understand that we could and should do something to heal these wounds.

The loss was terrible. We needed to listen closely, however, because the wounds and tears held wisdom for us. They helped us define the problem. They helped us know what could work and what was a stupid or superficial solution. They helped us have the energy to do the work, even when it meant confronting people we'd rather not confront.

Yes, you have to cross the threshold of a red door to enter. It would be crazy-making and disrespectful to not acknowledge that there is great loss in this world.

It would be equally damning to not see and enjoy the abundance that life has today.

But not any life. Life that is directed in pursuit of what is wholesome and loving; life that builds each other up and lets us pursue excellence and delight.

That is life worth pursuing. But you don't get there without learning from deep wounds that cry out for healing.

❦

The essays on the following pages share a blueprint from Rick's Place in hopes that they can inspire, support and engage others in the vital work of building communities, especially children's hearts, minds and imaginations. The work also helps us reconnect to each other in ways that are natural and fun, and that don't require you "use your words." Sometimes, words just get in the way.

Three quick points:

1. I do not share personally identifying information about service members or the roles they play in the US Military. My service was inspired by children who were like me when my family was in service (1960s-70s). Children do not have rank. They do have hearts that need to be loved and spirits that need to be encouraged.

2. I wished to provide a blueprint of the philosophy. However, the work we did was as a team. I can't and do not wish to take credit for others' work. I do wish to share my perspective of why we did what we did.

3. By February 2020, our community had become a sought-after partner by both military and civilian teams. Local leaders wanted to meet more, not less. The park was on solid financial footing (even with COVID) and a valuable voice of love and fun in a hard community. I had a hard choice to make. Each trip to Fayetteville was a four-hour round trip and I'd developed painful arthritis. I couldn't work harder and even if I could, that was not right for our community. It was time to step down. Local

leadership must run the park. The new leaders have deep passion for military families. I'm excited about its future, while at the same time I'm delighted to be working with other leaders to build communities that capable of love in the midst of COVID-19, death, destruction and despair.

For more about the Rick Herrema Foundation, please go to rhfnow.org. For more about me, go to allegrajordan.com.

Allegra Jordan
Chapel Hill, North Carolina

CHAPTER ONE

Sweet Enjoyment: George Washington's Dream

George Washington's farewell address concludes with a dream he held close to his heart:

"I anticipate with pleasing expectation that retreat, in which I promise myself to realize…the sweet enjoyment of partaking, in the midst of my fellow-citizens, the benign influence of good laws under a free government, the ever favorite object of my heart, and the happy reward, as I trust, of our mutual cares, labors, and dangers."

Washington's public service stretched 45 years. It was at times blisteringly traumatic, such as when he led his men into a massacre, saw them suffering at Valley Forge or was publicly attacked by his fellow insurrectionists as incompetent. His health was always precarious. As president he faced vicious partisan fighting, betrayal, rebellion and near financial ruin as he accrued large personal debts on tours to encourage citizens across the new country. As a farmer and slaveholder, he understood America had a long road ahead to form "a more perfect union."

Yet it was Washington's military and political service that created a world where peasant citizens could have their own farms, village and refuges to enjoy without fear. Washington was fond of quoting Micah 4:4,

> "They shall all sit under their own vines and under their own fig trees, and no one shall make them afraid."

Today, more than two hundred years later, this vision of "home" from our first general and president calls to warrior families from across the centuries. Flourishing, stable communities, Washington believed, redeem the extraordinary costs of warrior service.

Yet "coming home" is one of the most challenging parts of a warrior's journey.

Uptempo

"Leaving is hard. Returning is harder," is a phrase I often heard at work near Ft. Bragg, the largest US military installation by population. Service members move from the adrenaline-filled front line to the mundane activity required for friendship and family intimacy on the homefront. Some have forgotten what fun is. There is little space for fun in their "downrange" experience. Homefront friends and children worry if they will ever see their service member alive again. When the service member returns, kids may not recognize their mother or father. Everyone will have changed in the intervening days, months or year.

This leaving-returning-leaving cycle has accelerated since 9/11. That accelerated cycle is called an "uptempo" deployment cycle. The cycle has been set to "uptempo" the entirety of today's military children's life.

How do service members rebond and relearn the "splendor of attachment."[2]

Service members have little money or time to rebuild these intimate bonds. A US Army staff sergeant with six years of experience make less than $40,000 annually. A private with 2 years or less of experience makes around $19,000 a year. While service members receive housing and health allowances, these funds do not go far and 70% of military families do not live on post where many services are offered.[3]

Given these structural challenges, how is a service member to "come home"? (By "home" we mean, "the process of returning to the sphere of relationships the service member calls home.")

In the US, many services are provided for returning warriors and veterans. One unfilled need was space for positive play on the service member's own terms. So they built one.

The following essays outline a grassroots approach to reintegration developed by community members: soldiers and their families.

In sharing this approach, I remind communities about the power of community play to build capacity, leadership, resilience and powerful friendships.

A Space for Sweet Enjoyment

Warriors and their friends and families must have places to refresh themselves and renew their bonds with each other. They must be able to dictate the terms of how they accomplish this within the boundaries of a well-ordered community.

In 2014, US Army soldiers and their families bought an old horse farm 5.5 miles from Ft. Bragg. They converted the acreage to a rustic space where they could play, work on a shared project and reconnect with friends and families. The spot became known as "Rick's Place," and it is the pilot park for the Rick Herrema Foundation (RHF). The service members who founded RHF did so to honor the late Sgt. 1st Class Richard J. Herrema, a soldier and friend who died in Operation Iraqi Freedom.

For a cadre trained in service, such a space of sweet enjoyment is not a place of passive rest. It is a space of active service both given and received. They have gifts to give each other. Adults can mow lawns, clear underbrush, organize activities or read stories to kids. All but the youngest children can pick up pine straw or clean up the playgrounds. Service members can even use their special powers in fun ways, such as using a flame-thrower to light a bonfire of dead Christmas trees or build a trampoline platform for kids 18 feet up in the trees.

At Rick's Place we never called voluntarily offered service "therapy," even though such actions do have a healing benefit. We reject a pathology vocabulary when describing healthy human behavior.

If one has experienced terrible trauma ("love gone wrong[4]"), which all military families have or will experience, one still has gifts to give the community. One may have hearing loss – and probably will after being around explosives! But that does not eliminate one's ability to contribute. Building a community does not mean the service member does not go to a doctor. It means that the service member is not defined by his or her worst behavior, hearing loss or brain injury. The service member is much more than a list of pains and problems. The service member is a complex soul and she or he has gifts to share.

This includes one's own ability to change one's narrative from one of deficit to growth. As psychiatrist and PTSD pioneer Bessel van der Kolk argues, we have great capacities to invoke:

(1) Our capacity to destroy one another is matched by our capacity to heal one another. Restoring relationships and community is central to restoring well-being; (2) language gives us the power to change ourselves and others by communicating our experiences, helping us to define what

we know, and finding a common sense of meaning; (3) we have the ability to regulate our own physiology, including some of the so-called involuntary functions of the body and brain, through such basic activities as breathing, moving, and touching; and (4) we can change social conditions to create environments in which children and adults can feel safe and where they can thrive.[5]

Sometimes, seeing one's ability and gifts is hard. Life can be dangerous, discouraging, and lonely. Where challenges are prolonged or acute, one can de-skill him or herself, or believe one is helpless when one might not be so helpless.

"Learned helplessness" is way of looking at the world that says giving up is the most logical step forward. Learned helplessness explanations focus on facts that demonstrate a situation is pervasive, permanent, personal and isolated.

Here are some tough facts about war for military families.

- **Pervasive**. War's reach invades the rhythm of relationships. Even when soldiers are not deployed, alert status confines heavily-deployed forces' movements to a specific proximity near post.

- **Permanent**: America's 1.9 million active duty military children have never known a peacetime military. An additional 2 million Veterans' children have been born since 9/11 and they too have never experienced a peacetime military.[6]

- **Personal**: 50% of enlisted service members are married, and 70% of officers are married.[7] 42% of military personnel are parents.[8] For their children, a shadowy adversary is not after just anyone but one's parent. War is an existential threat.

- **Isolating**: 45% of youth of deployed parents report difficulties of not having people understand what they are going through around the deployment cycle.[9] According to the Vets4Warriors national support hotline, the top five types of calls each month to the hotline from Veterans and Active-Duty service members are about loneliness, depression, anxiety, relationships issues and financial concerns.[10]

- **Intense**: According to a 2018 Rand Study, heavily deployed soldiers make up about 13 percent of all soldiers but possess half the Army's deployment experience.[11] Deployment rates do vary in length and frequency by service. Some units are deployed for four months with three-month training cycles in-between deployments (often travel is required). Conventional deployments are 12-15 months. Single parents are not exempt from deployments.

These facts may make one pity military families, especially families of our Special Operations Forces who have borne the brunt of uptempo deployments since 9/11.

But what if military families do not want our pity? What if these very real sufferings are seen as tough growth experiences that help service families develop into America's next generation of great leaders?

Martin E. P. Seligman, the scientist who defined learned helplessness, made a second discovery soon after. Hope is also learned. This is good news!

The Rick Herrema Foundation is rooted in a vision that humans have gifts to give each other. Communal support, fun and a natural environment can embolden the bright human spirit alive in each person, and RHF wants that for those in our community.

I was also clear about two points:

1. Humans do not have simple on/off buttons to help us
    reset our nervous systems and change our paths. If we
    did, everyone would stop their self-defeating
    behaviors. Humans are complex. Wise counsel and
    positive support are required to help us move into a
    better future.

2. We must be careful how we define hope. There are
    many counterfeits. We do not need flimsy optimism or
    a superficial hope[12] or that promises a lot and delivers
    little. We want the real thing:
    - Hope of restoration to the circle of relationships we
      call home.
    - Hope to be well in body, mind and spirit.
    - Hope to laugh easily under a kind sun.
    - Hope to live with a clear and free heart.

This rich hope–which can and does deliver on its promises–
allows us to examine "What is going on?" with clear eyes. It
sees that loved ones can be hurt and even die in combat or
training. It sees that the soldier parent will leave and leave and
leave and some never return. This is all very true.

We need hope that we are not our worst days or injuries.
Real hope reminds us that there is marvelous delight and joy to
be had in life. We need hope that the "new normal" will bring
gifts with it. And that there may one day be a place of
reconnection and restoration, even if we have to build it
ourselves.

Real hope is spoken by this 21-year active-duty US Army
soldier who is also a father of five:

"The demands that modern military life places on the
family are staggering. Back-to-back deployments, intense
training cycles, and frequent cross-country moves are a fact
of life, and the families who are left at home are under

constant pressure to maintain some sense of sanity and stability in the service member's absence. RHF as an organization provides life-giving time and space to families in desperate need of it before, during and after the prolonged deployments and separations that characterize the military experience. Rick's Place, specifically, fills a need that has gone largely unaddressed by the many veteran and servicemember-focused organizations that exist nationwide: respite. Rick's Place provides my family with an environment where we can work together, play together and just BE together, in a beautiful outdoor setting, no strings attached. It's a place to unwind and disconnect from the pressures of everyday life, while forging bonds with other military families and the community that supports us that can sustain life long after we've left the grounds. It's a place where military spouses are honored and appreciated just as much as the servicemembers they support, and for whom they sacrifice. It's a place where we grow strong together, working side by side, exploring or enjoying new adventures. I love the look on my kids' faces when they pile out of the minivan and see the latest addition to the recreational scene at Rick's Place: zipline, obstacle course, bubble machine, nerf gun battleground—there's always a moment when they look back and me as if to say, "Dad, are you sure I'm allowed to do this?" The answer, at Rick's Place, is always yes.

This is the vision George Washington spent his whole life building for America. It is not just a gift to our military families. It is his gift to our Nation.

CHAPTER TWO

The Rick's Place Approach

Rick's Place provides free rustic playfields for members of the military family (broadly defined to include single soldiers, veterans and government contractors). Its mission is to provide stigma-free, fun, quality activities for the Military Family to support relationships and to build community. RHF believes that this approach helps keep healthy relationships healthy; can revive damaged relationships and helps model a wholesome and fun community that naturally entices people to participate.

RHF's approach adheres to five principles:

1. **No agenda**. Presume visitors are healthy and competent to narrate their own life journeys. Their company is to be enjoyed and not a "a set of problems to be solved." If visitors change, it's because they are capable of making their own decisions about their lives.

2. **Fun, quality activities in nature**. Rick's Place activities are curated to strengthen relationships before (or after) they face stress. The park is set in a natural setting for many reasons, including that service members tend to be comfortable with the outdoors and individuals tend to put away mobile devices when lifting heavy logs, water gun play, and Oobleck or mud immersion games. When I served, I sought to avoid "the entrapment of labels" or an expectation about any outcome. By keeping what we do as basic as possible ("RHF provides fields, nature, creek access, balls to

play with, books to read, etc."), the visitor keeps his or her agency and uses the labels he or she finds most helpful. This includes the right to reject Rick's Place community or accept it as helpful.

3. **We operate a cash-free park**. There is nothing for families to buy at Rick's Place during Work or Fun Day events (nor most other days). Money is a source of stress for many military families. RHF models how families can have fun without spending money. (RHF does charge for select events and day camps, especially where slots are limited as RHF has experienced people signing up for high-demand events and then not attending.)

4. **Volunteerism.** RHF operates a blended civilian/military community that is intergenerational and inter-ethnic. The park creates conditions where young kids, grandparents and all in-between can build our community through volunteering. This volunteering is meant to help model positive civic life.

   Importantly, RHF is not a rehabilitation service. It refers community service requests to local organizations whose purposes align with such requests, such as the Salvation Army.

5. **RHF enforces wholesome community norms and boundaries**.

   Visitors can expect that staff and other people at Rick's Place understand the unique stresses that military families experience. They will not have to educate others about what service members experience. They may find positive mentorship from staff and Board members who have "been there, done that." This cultural knowledge distinguishes RHF from many centers of worship, a YMCA or state park (all of which can provide excellent services).

RHF has encountered unruly or abusive visitors. It's rare, but it does happen. RHF will maintain its boundaries for the benefit of the community.

The ultimate desire at a respite park is that a visitor comes into our natural space out of curiosity and leaves with a different way of measuring his or her life.[13] In uncovering other possibilities for one's life, the idea of "home" is energized in a positive way. And when both "home" and "positive possibilities" are energized, service members can break the spell that work casts on them and enjoy ordinary life in the same way George Washington envisioned it: as a space of sweet enjoyment.

This transition may happen in one interaction or over the course of many visits. And it may not happen at all. The desire for positive outcomes can't interfere with visitors' actual experience.

RHF is an Intentional Community and not a State Park or YMCA

Rick's Place may look like a local public park. It's free. It has a nice pavilion and community garden. It has free libraries. The play spaces are stimulating and fun.

But Rick's Place is an approach to service member life. At its best, RHF supports a community that understands what military life requires and wants those involved in service careers to be able to come home and reintegrate successfully. Th RHF team members understand the military. Most were once the very boys, girls, teens, young adults and parents staff meet at Rick's Place each day.

What does success look like at Rick's Place?

Service members are surrounded by war and evaluation. At nearly every turn, they engaged in reviews, surveys, questionnaires and evaluations. As a result, RHF does not turn this space of enjoyment into a space of questionnaires.

So how do the park measure success?

The Rick Herrema Foundation does conduct off-site surveys and staff monitor direct visitor feedback. As executive director, I researched best practices and scoured the world for fun, quality activities. For instance, in a recent online survey developed with support from Pamela Wall, Ph.D., a retired US Navy psychiatrist, RHF rated 4.8/5 in "meets its mission" and had near perfect scores in terms of service and effectiveness.

We also quantify volunteer hours, outreach and financial goals. From April 2018- April 2019:

- By July 2019, RHF averaged approximately 500 visits per month, up from 250-300 visits per month in 2017.
- Leading members of the local and national military community affirmed that Rick's Place offers a distinct value proposition for the service member population.
- RHF formed and worked with an alliance of 30+ military service organizations to provide fun, quality programs for military families.
- RHF recorded more than 11,000 volunteers service hours.
- Monthly, RHF reached out to 50,000 military service members.
- RHF's major fundraising event contributed 90%+ of revenue raised to directly benefit military families.

- RHF's audit was deemed "The cleanest audit" the auditor had ever seen for a non-profit.
- RHF had financial reserves that would allow it to withstand deep economic disruption.

On a daily basis RHF looks for visual cues: relaxed shoulders, unclenched jaws and soft faces. The toddler screaming that they do not want to leave Rick's Place is also acceptable. Here are others:

- **Visible signs of enjoyment**: Witnessing people treating each other as gifts to be treasured and not as burdens.

- **Presence:** The visitor is with their loved one and not distracted (such as on a mobile device).

- **Physical attachment and affirmation**: Examples would be seeing service members and their loved ones engaged in positive support; loved ones hugging, holding hands; teens engaged in happy conversation; or a kid jumping into the welcoming arms of a parent. This is intimacy shared with loved ones which means, for this moment, the service member sees a loved one as interesting as his or her fellow work team or adrenaline-filled work. This also means the loved one affirms the service member is not a burden but a gift to one's heart.

This simple approach attempts to measure what can be measured in the moment without changing the moment.

Reintegration and the Playful Community

In a 2019 interview, play expert and scholar Thomas Henricks stated that "When one is in a positive community, one can feel the 'splendor of being attached.' Such an attachment can pull out better possibilities in a person and expand his or her circle of compassion. It can reaffirm powers outside of ourselves that are good."

While Rick's Place visitors can play individually, the mission orients RHF's activities to communal play, or "communitas," as he defines it. An example would be RHF's Fun or Work Days, or a shared community event such as a festival or concert.

Profession Henricks distinguishes communal play from individual play by its results. Play's emotional progression, Henricks writes, is *fun-exhilaration-gratification*. This can be a solitary act.

Communitas can provide a broader vision of play. People are willing "to seek feelings of transcendence that expand and integrate the self with others," and "to experience the re-creative or regenerative power of otherness."[14] The trajectory of a playful community event starts with anticipating a hopeful outcome. One then enters a stimulating community space, experiences positive recognition and support from the community and leaves with a sense of appreciation for what happened. Professor Henricks calls this emotion sequence *delight-joy-blessedness*.

At a Rick's Place Fun Day or Work Day, service members step into a space with other people who are experiencing what they are experiencing. Yet, because everyone is experiencing the military deployment cycle, they don't have to educate each other about the realities of military life. This is different from going to a public park, YMCA or even a family reunion where people in the room never understood war stress and often forget that one has it.[15]

Community play, concludes Professor Henricks, creates opportunities to "bond all participants through effusive expressions of support." Its pleasure "is not ours alone; it is something we share with our co-creators. Indeed, our enjoyment is magnified by their enthusiasm." Henricks' concludes, "Play of this type shifts questions of transformation and accomplishment from 'I' to 'we.'"[16]

RHF's own research bears this out. In a May 2018 survey of program activities "visiting with friends, "meeting new people" and communal events ranked as the most satisfying activities at Rick's Place.

According to UNC-Chapel Hill neuroscientist Darin Knapp, Ph.D., RHF's approach is more favorable than anything arising from today's neuroscience research labs. He stated:

> "Through the activities and opportunities that you provide /at Rick's Place/, you are helping people make new connections: cognitive, emotional, and arguably, physical connections involving neural circuitry. Your work surely impacts favorably on the mental health of your families as much or more than anything arising from our neuroscience research labs or clinics now and in the foreseeable future. And you are doing it in a naturalistic, intentional, approachable, and more comprehensive way where a completely mechanistic explanation of the benefits is unknown and perhaps unknowable."

CHAPTER THREE

Tug-o-War:
Life challenges are not PTSD

Every human must answer the question, "Do I want to be healthy?" many times in life. It is one of life's most important questions, as it makes possible the rest of life. No one is exempt from this question.

At the Rick Herrema Foundation I sought to provide the conditions for individuals to respond, "Yes!"

What does a "Yes!" look like? It's helpful to have a checklist. Theodore Ryan, Ph.D., is the consulting professor of business ethics at Duke University. His background is in organizational psychology, moral philosophy, anthropology and religion. Professor Ryan lists these data points as evidence of a flourishing human:[17]

- A strong positive sense of self
- Compelling purpose greater than self-interest
- A circle of healthy relationships (from intimate to casual)
- Connection to a healthy community
- A developed moral character (the capacity to act on moral impulses)

- Self-awareness and other-awareness (including mindfulness and empathy)
- Full deployment of gifts in a way that is aligned with purpose and positive character
- A sense of transcendence: appreciate mystery, wonder & play; celebrate the goods of life; a creative imagination
- Resilience: transforming adversity into growth; optimism and growth motivation
- A sense of joy; a capacity for fun and enjoyment

If the person has a firm "No" inside, the community soon finds out. That person drains others of their joy and resources. In some ways the person is committing slow-motion suicide. Unfortunately, this giving up is not as private as one may think. Children are acutely aware when a parent does not meet their reasonable needs. The child depends on the parent for survival. When a parent is not able to provide, children may maladapt through codependent behaviors and/or a spectrum of averse, anxious attachment styles.[18]

Some people are honestly unsure if they have a "Yes" or "No" inside. There are many reasons for this. A person may be coping with a terrible situation. He or she may have never seen a healthy community or been in a healthy relationship. A person may have been conditioned to believe community support is "weak," that healthy communities and relationships are fakes, frauds and cruel myths designed to cause pain. A person may be on the verge of giving up, seeing that there is no end in sight to the misery of the current situation. This does not mean they have a firm "No" inside of them. This means they can be persuaded.

For instance, in late fall of 2017 a rail-thin woman came to watch her teen sons compete on a free obstacle course the founder of the America Ninja Warrior Series designed and built for a weekend of fun, quality activities. Her eyes were often tear-rimmed, though she was looking at a grand scale exhibit of families enjoying each other's company while competing on a world-class course. A person mentioned that we had an art exhibit at our Welcome Center. She asked to go see it, and a staff member accompanied her. She told the staff member that her husband had been killed downrange just that summer. She came out for the competition because she wanted her children to see life goes on. She wanted to live and not be a shut in. She wanted to be off post. She thanked the staff for the work and asked to come back one day.

Even if one is healthy, there comes a time when all humans need, appreciate and enjoy support. Even Nobel prize laureate Albert Schweitzer observed,

> "At times our own light goes out and is rekindled by a spark from another person. Each of us has cause to think with deep gratitude of those who have lighted the flame within us."[19]

Case study:
Tug-O-War between "Yes" and "No"
at Rick's Place

Roughly twice-a-month, before COVID-19, Rick's Place issued invitations to active duty service members, their loved ones and our wider community. One invitation is to help build the park at an event called "Work Day." The second is for a day of organized play called "Fun Day."

Under a gray January sky in 2018, the Rick's Place team launched its first "Brawny Bunch Olympics." We expected to see rustic competitions like Tug-o-War and log toss. We didn't expect to see the battle between a mother's "Yes" and "No" played out in front of us.

"Get over here!" called Gunner, the aptly-named adult son of a gifted sniper. On that gray January day, Gunner waved to the pre-teens standing in line for the Rick's Place zipline. "Tug-o-war! Come on!" Gunner called, pointing to the dormant West Gardens field about 100 yards away.

A pair of young boys stood with Gunner waving the American and the Olympic flags while the opening theme of the 2018 Brawny Bunch Olympics played on our loudspeaker that cool January Saturday morning. Suddenly a wave of toddlers zoomed behind the flag bearers and lustily marched to the mammoth tug-of-war rope in the garden. Parents, alert that their kids were no longer in collar-grabbing reach, hustled over to the parade line, many still in conversation. The older kids' curiosity got the best of them. They abandoned the zipline and sprinted to catch up with the parade.

The parade came to a halt around the rope.

"Gather round!" called Gunner to the crowd of 125 soldiers, spouses, friends and kids. He was a medium-built, strong-as-an-ox, 26-year old who ran programs and facilities for Rick's Place from 2017-2019. He was also "Kid Velcro." Walk Gunner across a field and young kids would cling to him like grass burrs.

"Before we start we're going to do a real warrior's war cry. So circle-out, lock arms and repeat after me!"

Quickly the crowd got into position, many adults on their knees so they could help out the younger kids. Arm-in-arm, the crowd began to sway.

"Tocka-tocka!"
A few kids called out "Tocka-tocka."
"Louder!" called Gunner.
"TOCKA-TOCKA!" came the full-throated response.

"CHING-CHING!" yelled Gunner. Suddenly the park was one voice, echoing nonsense words with gusto back at the game's leader.

And so began the 2018 Brawny Bunch Olympics. Strangers engaged in a communal dance that made sense for them: military families, many of who will not dance in public. But they will commit to a family war cry that made nearly everyone hoarse even before the games started. (The next month, some parents and kids told us they just come just for War Cry.)

In the midst of the crowd, though, one family looked different. The mom wore a black hoodie, a scowl on her face and yelled at her kids. Her kids were disheveled and pale.

We had seen this family at a prior "Fun Day," a monthly family field day we held to provide a few hours of fun plus a modest free lunch for families. The sun, fresh air, warm meal, and even the cute puppies who visited couldn't impact their demeanor.

And yet, the family came out when they could have stayed home. This was a good sign.

After the war cries, Gunner lined up kids, about twenty on a side, for tug-o-war. The kids battled it out while adults cheered them on from the sidelines. "Heave! Heave!" we all called. Finally one side pulled the rope past the winning marker and victory was declared. "Rematch!" the kids demanded - and they got one.

Just about that time, the sun came out. Men donned their sunglasses and took the rope. Sturdy gals then pulled an epic, hard fought contest and rematch. The angry mother joined in on the line. The first time her side lost. But a rematch was demanded and granted. And this time, her side won.

Just after that victory – where no prizes were given – our staff members saw her smile and her face soften. For the first time in two "Fun Days" we heard her laugh. Soon, the foreboding black hoodie came off to reveal a plain, gray t-shirt and jeans. She looked visibly different: relaxed and happier. Her children noticed it too. They drew physically closer to her.

Our staff last saw the mother and child at the edge of a golden field, child in lap. The mother stroked the child's hair in a moment of peace, oblivious to the rest of the people in the fields along with them. The sun and fresh air were their friends. The family–for this moment, this wisp of time – re-bonded.

RHF's approach is rooted in psychologist Carl Rogers' observations about conditions humans need to do their best work: genuine interest, positive regard, empathy, warmth, trust. Our approach is also rooted in a love that is not blind, but a love that sees people for who they are and does not try to remake those people in our own image.

Why do hundreds of people each month visit Rick's Place? What is the question that this space answers? Those answers will be as different as the individuals who come. More often than not, the root cause is the same: some spark of hope and faith is inside of them. Somewhere inside they know that an imperfect but positive community may be able to help them flourish in the face of war.

This does not mean it was easy to come out to Rick's Place. It means that the need was great enough and that the warrior prioritized fun.

One Soldier and Family Readiness Group organizer wrote to RHF in 2018:

"Our unit is part of the 82nd Airborne Division. To say our paratroopers and their families have a busy schedule would be the understatement of the century! To be able to come to Rick's place and relax as a family (our immediate family but also our troop family) was wonderful. Our kids immediately gravitated toward the obstacle course and had a blast on the zip line. Younger children were able to play at the park, while a few kids played soccer and the adults competed in corn hole. Toward the end of the evening we were all able to gather around the fire pit and enjoy a s'more together (or two or three!) Thank you, Rick's Place, for your support of the military families at Fort Bragg. It means more than words can express!"

A Note about PTSD

At Rick's Place we were not professional therapists. We tried to be friends. To us, friends:

- See each other,
- Encourage the heart, mind and spirit,
- Call each other on unproductive behavior, and
- Allow the friend to do the same for us. Friendship is a two-way street.

If a visitor sought therapeutic resources and asked us for referrals, we would do our best to refer people to professionals in our community.

We also did not make assumptions. If a soldier just got off a plane eight hours ago from a war zone and was now at Rick's Place, the soldier may have a heightened sense of situational awareness. This does not mean the person has PTSD. This means that a soldier was trained well for war and has just moved between war and peace. It's a normal response for people who have been well-trained to stay alive in a war zone.

Post-Traumatic Stress Disorder (PTSD) occurs in 11-20% of recent veterans. It occurs in 7-8% of the US population.[20] PTSD's symptoms can include reliving the event, becoming hypervigilant, angry outbursts, avoiding places that one can't control and negative changes in beliefs and feelings.

PTSD can and should be addressed with professional support through a variety of solutions that help a person digest overwhelming and negative experiences.

Unfortunately, the therapeutic language of PTSD has permeated the public imagination to the point some service members feel something must be wrong with them if they do not have PTSD![21]

One is reminded of a story told about a Christian Sunday School class. The teacher asked the children, "What is grey, has a furry tail and gathers nuts in winter?" The child responds, "It seems like a squirrel to me but I think I'm supposed to say Jesus."

Sometimes life feels unbearable. That happens to everyone. Feeling that way does not mean a person has a disorder. It does mean that person has a growth opportunity and choices to make about purpose, values and how to solve that challenge. It does mean a person will once again say either 'yes' or 'no' to life.

CHAPTER FOUR

The Splendor of Outdoor Play: A light to navigate the landscape of the human heart

America's service members are trained in land navigation. They can read a map, shoot an azimuth and get where it is vital for them and their team to be.

But the rugged terrain of reintegration is not found on a map. It changes each time a family or friends endure stress. If a family wants to be healthy, how do they lead and navigate across this invisible, powerful landscape? What are its guiding landmarks?

Landmarks for the Human Heart

American's service members are perfectly capable of understanding Russian writer Fyodor Dostoevsky. About 150 years ago, Dostoevsky observed three *interdependent* landmarks for "heart navigation."

1. **Physical play**. "It is sometimes very pleasant, too, to smash things."[22]

2. **Beauty**. "Beauty will save the world."[23]

3. **Golden moments**. "You must know that there is nothing higher and stronger and more wholesome and good for life in the future than some good memory, especially a memory of childhood, of home. People talk to you a great deal about your education, but some good, sacred memory, preserved from childhood, is perhaps the best education. If a man carries many such memories with him into life, he is safe to the end of his days, and if one has only one good memory left in one's heart, even that may sometime be the means of saving us."[24]

At RHF, each landmark supported the conditions for human flourishing.

Landmark 1: How Smashing and Other Forms of Play Support Flourishing & Reintegration

According to the Oxford English Dictionary, the verb play means to "Engage in activity for enjoyment and recreation rather than a serious or practical purpose."[25]This is a vast simplification of an ambiguous idea.[26] As play scholar Erving Goffman observed, 'Whatever play is, it always runs parallel to our lives, serving as a respite from ordinary events and a lesson on how life can actually be better than it is."[27] Professor Thomas Henricks also adds that play in his works, and most scholarly works, presumes play pulls out one's better possibilities and is not hazing, bullying or domination with intent to demean another person.

Numerous studies document the complex nature of play and its benefits and challenges. Articles and insights from the

National Institute for Play, The Strong (a research institute and museum dedicated to play), *The American Journal of Play*, and important books by thought leaders Thomas Henricks, Brian Sutton-Smith, David Elkins, Scot Eberle and other scientists, researchers and sociologists articulate the science, benefits and risks of play.

Professor Thomas Henricks describes play as one of four pathways of experience, the other three being work, ritual and community engagement. At Rick's Place, every month we invite people to all four, but through the primary lens of play.

This essay focuses on qualitative results of the fun, quality activities done in nature and in community. It shows how these activities support warrior reintegration, framing a positive culture, building a positive community, exploring leadership roles and promoting resilience.

Smashing things, and other forms of visceral play, can feel liberating. Sometimes it also feels necessary. The idea is to get out of one's rational brain and let the body have a life of its own within certain bounds. (If, however, one smashes another person's peace of mind, the forecast for family reconciliation looks stormy. At Rick's Place, we knew the difference!)

Play at Rick's Place was not limited to just smashing. Visitors are given choices of what kind of play they wish to engage in that include exploring, reading, rocking on a front porch, arts & crafts, or playing with the balls in a sports equipment shed. Henricks categorizes these different types of play as exploration, interpretation, construction and dialogue.[28] Each of these types of play teach one about different types of human interactions in the wider world.

Here are two examples of how the healthy exuberance of smashing, sloshing and other forms of messiness have been engaged at Rick's Place. They engage all four forms of play that Professor Henricks describes. They also include elements of community building, work and ritual, ways humans experience life.

Mud Kitchen Time

For two years, a military wife and mother of nine children carefully studied what kind of space would serve young families at Rick's Place, especially the mothers of young children. She organized the creation of a "play kitchen" with shaded space for parents to sit while children engaged in make-believe house play. One vital element for children was the inclusion of a source of mud and water.

When RHF staff clean up the kids' mud kitchen staff do wonder, "Can't mud kitchens be tidy?"

But staff hearts melted when a mother called RHF, saying,

"I know you all are having a lot of construction. But tomorrow is our last day in Fayetteville. We're being transferred to a new post. I asked my girls what they wanted to do, and they said, 'Play at your mud kitchen one last time before we leave!' May we come out?"

"Yes. Of course!" said RHF staff.

Smashing social distance with humor

The Joke Doctor concept is simple. Set up a table and a chair. Sit behind the table. Put up a sign that says "Joke Doctor." Have a sack of Groucho Marx glasses with the eyebrows, nose and mustache.

The first time working with Joke Doctor at Fun Day, kids of different ages came to the table, curious about what this Joke Doctor was. A small crowd of kids quickly gathered once they realized the topic was jokes. A three-year-old ran to

get her mother to explain what a joke was because she needed
one for the Joke Doctor.

The staff member manning the table either laughed or
helped them with their joke. Soon, kids asked to be the joke
doctors themselves.

A seasoned battalion commander came over to the
table. By the time he arrived, three kids and an adult created a
whole staff of joke doctors. Lori, 5, was the youngest.

"Tell us your joke!" she said.

"Why is a tomato the stupidest fruit?" the commander
asked.

"Why?" we ask.

"Because it doesn't get that it doesn't belong in a fruit
salad."

The tween, teen and staff member had no reaction.

Lori doubled over with laughter. Tears came to her
eyes. She sighed heavily as she stopped laughing.

"Your joke makes an impression with the younger
set," the staff member said.

"Just the younger set?" asked the commander.

"All good data," the staff member said, handing him a
pair of Groucho Marx glasses for his efforts. He popped them
on, showed his wife (who laughed), and they allowed RHF
staff to take a photo of them.

Play can look deceptively simple. But a lot may be going on inside a person that is teaching him or her about life, relationships, community, leadership and resilience.

As play expert Brian Sutton-Smith wrote in his essay, "Play as Emotional Survival,"

"The expressive, regulative character of play is its most adaptive general feature. The mutative reflexive and reflective emphases for players become the playful everyday attempts to adjust the relationships between their emotions and the skills and rules of the game they pursue. The learning of these skills and rules, the forms of gamesmanship requires a certain degree of social complexity, which in the long run offers the players a series of insights into the complex fiber of everyday social life, including its politics. …In short, the social complexity of our games promise an understanding at the same level that helps maintain our subsequent civil existence."[29]

He concludes with a note about resilience:

"From watching children play over the years, I have been impressed with the hardships of the intense learning required for them to continue to engage in various kinds of play. Unfortunately, the joy children express in their play often conceals from adults how hard they have to work at gaining the social skills and physical abilities to allow them to have so much fun."[30]

Landmark 2: Beauty

Beauty is not often at the top of the list of things a service member asks for in his or her life. However, beauty is one of the three things the ancients said were required for a flourishing life. (Truth, goodness and beauty.)[31]   Yet when service members experience beauty, they may realize how much they have missed beauty's presence.

We are clear: the military is a large place and not everyone enjoys the beauty of nature. But many do like fresh air, seeing wild animals and an abundant garden. Some enjoy the frisson of fear at knowing they may see a snake, and the joy of seeing the red-tailed hawks soaring overhead and hearing the frog chorus come out at dusk.

It's this person who, upon seeing something they respect and love and find beautiful, relaxes and smiles. With a mere glance–no words, no gestures, nothing but their own vision– they are taken to a different place in their heart where their burdens shift and life becomes lighter.

One can play in standard military housing, at a park patrolled by an armed guard or even in a gray cubicle. But George Washington had in mind something different when he cast a vision of "sweet enjoyment" for members of the military family.

Kirsten Brunson is a retired military judge whose husband is still on active duty. While stationed at Ft. Bragg, she came to Rick's Place with her son, who loves to simply run. She reflected,

"There are wonderful programs at Fort Bragg for soldiers and their families. But it's on Fort Bragg. You're around soldiers all day. This gets you away from all of that, so you can take a deep breath and relax. You're not going to run into somebody in uniform. You're not worried about who outranks you. You're just out here with your family, enjoying nature, enjoying each other in a peaceful setting. It's built as a respite, and it really is."[32]

Part of that respite is the respite provided freely by nature. Nature matters. As priest and poet John O'Donohue writes,

"The ancient rhythms of the earth have insinuated themselves into the rhythms of the human heart. The earth is not outside us; it is within: the clay from where the tree of the body grows. When we emerge from our offices, rooms and houses, we enter our natural element. We are children of the earth: people to whom the outdoors is home. Nothing can separate us from the vigour and vibrancy of this inheritance. In contrast to our frenetic, saturated lives, the earth offers a calming stillness. Movement and growth in nature takes time. The patience of nature enjoys the ease of trust and hope. There is something in our clay nature that needs to continually experience this ancient, outer ease of the world. It helps us remember who we are and why we are here."[33]

Case Study

A Visit from Col. Schrumpf

Col.(ret) Ray Schrumpf was a POW for five years in Vietnam. He was kept in inhumane conditions. He lived near Ft. Bragg until his death in 2019. Shortly before he died, he told me he still had nightmares about his days in captivity.

He came to Rick's Place one "Fun Day" driven by members of the local Rolling Thunder motorcycle group.
Col Schrumpf told a member of Rick's Place staff, "I got out of the truck and walked into this field. I felt a burden lift. I felt at peace."

A small crowd gathered around Col. Schrumpf. He listened to soldiers' and volunteers' stories. He shared his journey of healing and was open about how he struggled with brutal memories. He mentioned he had just started therapy in his late 70s, and talked about how much it had helped.

At one point he said he loved dogs but didn't have one. Fortunately, therapy-puppies-in-training were on site courtesy of Continuing the Mission (CtM). The puppies trotted over to lick Col. Schrump's hands and to sit by him as he visited on that sunny morning. Before he left, he mentioned how he would like to come back and sit out in nature with us again.

Landmark 3: Golden Moments

Golden moments that Dostoevsky recommends are desired end-states. A "golden moment" is a specific, wonderful wholesome memory one can recall with great pleasure. Recollection of such a moment may change one's heartrate, breathing and soften one's facial expression.

For each person, a golden moment is personal and often eternal. Forcing a golden moment to happen is like trying to force oneself to go to sleep. The more your force, the more elusive it is. Yet golden moments do sometimes surprise us and, when they do, they make life marvelous.

Here are four examples:

Chupacabras for Mother's Day, 2019

Rick's Place has "massive, interactive story time" from time to time. On Mother's Day weekend a young Special Forces wife beamed after she and her daughter dressed as Chupacabras, fought off "Orcs" with our Nerf gun arsenal (HADES XVIIIs for the Nerf connoisseur) and then pelted each other with water balloons to clean off their make-up. The mother told the Rick's Place Volunteer Manager, "I just had the best day with my daughter. We ran around and played without any phones! We laughed so much. This was the best Mother's Day present I could get!"

Healing Memories, 2018

"We made life-long friendships through Rick's Place family. We miss being a part of it. However, there is not a day that goes by that we don't think about you all. We cannot wait until we are stationed back at Bragg, so that we can reconnect."

-MaDonna, military spouse

Waking Up to Life

In Spring 2018, a soldier's son was admitted to a psychiatric ward on suicide watch. He was released the next week. Surprisingly, six weeks later, the young man came with his father and step-mother to RHF's June Work Day. The son engaged in manual labor alongside his father. The young man found he liked using his hands. The next week, the young man got up early to come to Rick's Place on our field mowing day. All day in the hot sun the young man mowed fields. His only condition for volunteering was that that he could hang out with facilities manager on breaks. The boy's step-mom reported, "I have never seen him wake himself up so early, get so dirty or look so happy."

An Army Ranger's New Dream for Himself

In 2017, a young soldier working his way through a military qualifications course came out to Rick's Place. He had asked where he could be in a positive environment and volunteer during his down time. The soldier, we'll call him Ben, was directed to RHF by the battalion commander who had told the tomato joke noted in the above section on 'smashing.".

Ben self-identified as an introvert. He wanted to work with as few people as possible. He started by painting a room in our Welcome Center. The next week we asked him to move some heavy tree trunks with two other soldiers. We saw him next at a Fun Day, where he volunteered to help set up but left before the kids got to the park. He then disappeared for several months, we learned due to both training and an injury.

When he showed up again, he volunteered to come to Fun Day and this time he stayed after the kids arrived. He was asked to form a "Wall of Soldiers" to take on kids in a game of tag. "Let the kids win?" he asked. "Oh, they'll win. Just try not to lose. Height is a disadvantage in this game."

Soon, Ben helped with every Fun Day activity, from parking, to running the activities, to set up and tear down. Every kid wanted to jump on him, ride with him in the 4x4, learn how to shoot targets from him or challenge him in a game of chase.

The day came in 2019 when Ben received a promotion and orders to transfer to his new assignment. When he told RHF's team he was going to leave there was not a dry eye around Rick's Place.

Ben said his time at RHF had helped him refine his future goals. After he was done with the US Army, he wanted to settle down, have kids and become a good father and husband. This, he said, was a new goal for him.

This change took place without a heart-to-heart, in fact, no one ever discussed the matter with him. The change was done over time. It was an inside job: Ben owned he wanted to change.

We know that one day some kid will be lucky to call him 'Dad.'

As the inventor of the inkblot test, Hermann Rorschach, wrote to Leo Tolstoy,

"To be understood from the heart, without formalities and tricks and heaps of erudite words, that is what we are all looking for."

There are no golden moments without the heart being touched. This may happen due to a connection with the spiritual world, nature, an animal such as a horse or dog, or another human being. The moment helps one feel deep in the bones what it means to be heard, loved and, for that moment, that life was good. When one has this felt sense of how good life can be, one may be able to recall that the rest of one's days. This is what Dostoevsky meant by saying golden moments can be the means of a person's salvation.

We the People: Service Member, Citizen, Community and Country

General George Washington wrote a prescient letter in 1775 to a member of the New York Legislature:

> "May your every wish be realized in the success of America, at this important and interesting Period; and be assured that the every exertion of my worthy Colleagues and myself will be equally extended to the re-establishment of Peace and Harmony between the Mother Country and the Colonies, as to the fatal, but necessary, operations of War. When we assumed the Soldier, we did not lay aside the Citizen; and we shall most sincerely rejoice with you in that happy hour when the establishment of American Liberty, upon the most firm and solid foundations, shall enable us to return to our Private Stations in the bosom of a free, peaceful and happy Country."[34]

As noted in these brief pages, the challenge of creating and maintaining a free, peaceful and happy space upon returning home requires both citizen and soldier working together in intentional community.

When they do, America benefits. RHF's motto is, "Strong family. Strong Military. Strong Nation." Service members age out of the military. Service members and their families take their abilities to build strong, wholesome relationships to new jobs and new communities. Their leadership and resilience can help communities navigate important landmarks of the heart no matter the terrain.

RHF also believes that the lessons learned can be applied in areas where reintegration is just assumed, such as when a person returns from a long work trip or college. There are also tough adjustments, such as when a person comes home from rehabilitation or from detention within the justice system.

Perhaps a military family said it best:

"To us, Rick's Place is our happy place: a place in which we positively connect with the community. We reinforce the importance of team work, responsibility and be actively healthy. It is a place to connect even more as a family and make more memories. Thanks to Rick's staff for being so welcoming."

– Johanna, JJ & Ecktor

Selected Readings

Non-Fiction

Henricks, Thomas. *Play and the Human Condition.* (Urbana: University of Illinois Press), 2015.

Hoge, Charles. *Once a Warrior Always a Warrior: Navigating The Transition From Combat To Home--Including Combat Stress, Ptsd, And Mtbi.* (US: Lyons Press), 2010.

Kolk, Bessel van der. *The Body Keeps the Score.* (New York: Viking Press) 2014.

Marsh, Charles. *The Beloved Community: How Faith Shapes Social Justice, from the Civil Rights Movement to Today.* (US: Basic Books), 2006.

Searls, Damion. *The Inkblots: Hermann Rorschach, His Iconic Test, and the Power of Seeing.* (New York: Crown) 2017.

Sutton-Smith, Brian. *Play for Life.* (New York: The Strong), 2017.

Tedeschi, Richard, and Bret Moore. *The Post-Traumatic Growth Workbook.* (US: New Harbinger Publications), 2016.

Epic Poetry about the Journey to Well-being

Guite, Malcolm, *Mariner: A Voyage with Samuel Taylor Coleridge,* (London: Hodder & Stoughton), 2017.

Homer, trans. Emily Wilson, *The Odyssey.* (New York: WW Norton), 2017.

Heaney, Seamus, "Crediting Poetry, Nobelprize.org, https://www.nobelprize.org/prizes/literature/1995/heaney/lecture/ accessed August 1, 2019.

Acknowledgements

I was a midwife to Rick's Place, but I am not the community. Community members are listed on the RHF site at www.rhfnow.org. These essays share my perspective. Their stories are for them to tell, not for me to share. Having heard some of them, I hope and encourage them to share their incredible journeys in print as they reflect some of the best America has to offer.

I thank the incredible patriots who funded and built Rick's Place including those who wish to remain anonymous and those I can thank publicly, including Mark and Emily Fauk, Joel and Nancy Kobert, Pixie and Rich Keating, Mrs. Jacqueline Mars, and John and Marsha Messervey. Their generosity makes a big difference, year-in and year-out. As Dolly Parton said, "It takes a lot of money to look this cheap." (We call it 'rustic,' and 'frugal' at Rick's Place.)

Rick's Place went through a particularly fragile stage when I first served as executive director. Many hands helped, some that can't be named here. I am especially grateful to for the above-and-beyond service of the families of Katherine Barnett and Kimberly Weimer. I am also grateful for Frank Eng whose welcome embrace helped Rick's Place integrate with the military community.

I thank all who gave feedback on early versions of this essay collection. I thank the many service families who contributed their stories to this work.

I thank my family. My husband, Theodore Ryan, built Rick's Place alongside me. My brother, military historian Jonathan W. Jordan, signed and sent his best-selling books to RHF supporters to thank them on my behalf. My mother created art for Rick's Place and never would fail to support a veteran I asked her to invite to her Blue Ridge mountain cabin.

For more about the Rick Herrema Foundation, visit www.rhfnow.org. For more about Allegra Jordan, please go to www.allegrajordan.com.

About the Author

Allegra Jordan served as the Executive Director of the Rick Herrema Foundation, 2017-2020. Named an "Architect of Change" by Maria Shriver, Allegra has worked on the front lines of innovation work in numerous industries, 17 countries and on five continents. Her articles, essays and cases have appeared in USA TODAY, Harvard Business School Press, *Huffington Post*, Duke University's Faith and Leadership.com and other publications. Her best-selling World War I novel is *The End of Innocence* (Sourcebooks, 2014), and her poetry collection is *We Interrupt These Wars* (2019). Allegra holds an MBA from Harvard Business School and a leadership coaching certificate from Georgetown University.

Today she is a leadership coach, author and social entrepreneur, launching a public benefit corporations to support building superior teams on the twin pillars of love and excellence.

www.allegrajordan.com

Endnotes

[1] Fyodor, Dostoevsky, *The Brothers Karamazov,* trans. Constance Garnett (New York, The Macmillan Company, 1922, 836, *accessed* July 21, 2019. *//books.google.com/books/about/The_Brothers_Karamazov.html?id =mMNKAAAAYAAJ&printsec=frontcover&source=kp_read_button #v=onepage&q&f=false.*

[2] Author interview with play expert Thomas Hendricks, July 2019.

[3] Jim Garamone, "Military Children Serve, Too." *U.S. Department of Defense*, accessed July 21, 2019, //dod.defense.gov/News/Article/Article/719407/military-children-serve-too/.

[4] Maria Popova, "The Science of How Our Minds and Our Bodies Converge in the Healing of Trauma," *Brain Pickings,* accessed July 21, 2019, https://www.brainpickings.org/2016/06/20/the-body-keeps-the-score-van-der-kolk/. Bessel van der Kolk, *The Body Keeps the Score*, (New York: Viking Press, 2014).

[5] Maria Popova, "The Science of How Our Minds and Our Bodies Converge in the Healing of Trauma," *Brain Pickings,* https://www.brainpickings.org/2016/06/20/the-body-keeps-the-score-van-der-kolk/, accessed July 21, 2019.

[6] Military Child Education Coalition, *College, Career and Life Readiness for Military and Veteran Children.* 2015. 5. Print.

[7] "Get to know your Military," *U.S. Department of Defense,* accessed July 21, 2019, https://www.defense.gov/KnowYourMilitary/.

[8] U. S. Department of Defense, *Report on the Impact of Deployment of Members of the Armed Forces on Their Dependent Children: Report to the Senate and House Committees on Armed Services Pursuant to National Defense Authorization Act for Fiscal Year 2010 Section 571," U.S. Department of Defense*, October 2010, accessed July 21, 2019, https://download.militaryonesource.mil/12038/MOS/Reports/Report

 _to_Congress_on_Impact_of_Deployment_on_Military_Children.p
df.
[9]Anita Chandra, et. al., "Views from the Homefront: The
Experience of Youth and Spouses from Military Families," Rand
Health Q. 2011 Spring; 1(1): 12.,
https://www.ncbi.nlm.nih.gov/pmc/articles/PMC4945219/, accessed
August 1, 2019.
[10] Lloyd Deans of Vets4Warriors Hotline, Interview with Author,
February 2019.
[11] Jennie Wenger, Caolion O'Connell, Linda Cottrell,
*Examination of Recent Deployment Experience Across the Services
and Components,* Rand Corporation, 2018, accessed July 21, 2019,
//www.rand.org/pubs/research_reports/RR1928.html?adbsc=social_
20180320_2212921&adbid=975928167633334272&adbpl=tw&adb
pr=22545453.
[12] Superficial hope examples include the purchases of consumer
goods (e.g. 'If you buy X you will feel great!'), temporary numbing
agents ('Play this addictive game; drink Y or eat X and life will be
good.'), false promises of intimacy ('If you had the right person in
your life then life would be great so click here…'), spiritual egotism
('If you breathe correctly or pray correctly you will get everything
you want.'), or empty intellectual promises ("If you just get another
degree or read the right books then life will be all right.") All of
these promises have some kernel of truth in them, but overall are
very thin things to base one's hope on.
[13] This invokes a statement by master British gardener Monty Don
who said that people come to a great garden with a sense of curiosity
or for pleasure but one hopes that they leave with a different way to
measure their lives. "The South." *Monty Don's Italian Gardens.*
Netflix, 2011. Television.
[14] Thomas Henricks, *Play and the Human Condition*, (Urbana:
University of Illinois Press, 2015), 59.
[15] Author interview with military spouse Katherine Barnett, 2018.
[16] Thomas Henricks, *Play and the Human Condition*, (Urbana:
University of Illinois Press, 2015), 58-67.
[17] Theodore Ryan, *Flourishing Humans* [PowerPoint slides.], 2019.
[18] Attachment in adults, (n.d.), In *Wikipedia*, accessed July 21, 2019,
https://en.wikipedia.org/wiki/Attachment_in_adults.
[19] Albert Schweitzer Quotes, (n.d.) *BrainyQuote,* accessed July 21,
2019,https://www.brainyquote.com/quotes/albert_schweitzer_40228
2.

[20]U.S. Department of Veterans Affairs, "How Common is PTSD in Veterans?" PTSD: National Center for PTSD, accessed July 21, 2019, //www.ptsd.va.gov/understand/common/common_veterans.asp.

[21] C.J. Chivers, "An Army Vet Comes to Terms with not Having PTSD," *New York Times Magazine*, accessed July 21, 2019, //www.nytimes.com/2019/05/31/magazine/army-veteran-ptsd-trauma.html.

[22] Fyodor Dostoyevsky. (n.d.) In *Wikipedia*, accessed July 21, 2019, //en.wikiquote.org/wiki/Fyodor_Dostoyevsky.

[23] Alexandr Solzhenitsyn, *Nobel Lecture*, (NobelPrize.org. Nobel Media AB, 1970), accessed July 21, 2019, https://www.nobelprize.org/prizes/literature/1970/solzhenitsyn/lecture/.

[24] Fyodor, Dostoevsky, *The Brothers Karamazov,* trans. Constance Garnett (New York, The Macmillan Company, 1922, 836, *accessed July 21, 2019,* *//books.google.com/books/about/The_Brothers_Karamazov.html?id=mMNKAAAAYAAJ&printsec=frontcover&source=kp_read_button#v=onepage&q&f=false*.

[25] Merrian Webster, s.v. "Play," accessed July 21, 2019, //www.lexico.com/en/definition/play.

[26] Play expert Brian Sutton-Smith wrote a book called *The Ambiguity of Play* in which he explored more than 100 concepts that characterize play. He concluded, "Clearly, play was either extremely diverse or extremely complex." Brian Sutton-Smith, *Play for Life*, (New York: The Strong, 2017), 65.

[27]Brian Sutton-Smith, *Play for Life*, (New York: The Strong, 2017), 67.

[28] Thomas Henricks, "Theme and Variation: Arranging Play's Forms, Functions, and "Colors," *American Journal of Play*, 10 no. 2, (Winter 2018).

[29] Brian Sutton-Smith, *Play for Life*, (New York: The Strong, 2017), 89.

[30]Brian Sutton-Smith, *Play for Life*, (New York: The Strong, 2017), 89.

[31] Transcendentals (n.d.) In *Wikipedia,* accessed July 21, 2019. //en.wikipedia.org/wiki/Transcendentals.

[32] Yonat Shimron, "Rick's Place offers military families a place to gather for community and fun," *Faith & Leadership,* Duke University, September 18, 2019, accessed July 21, 2019. https://www.faithandleadership.com/ricks-place-offers-military-families-place-gather-community-and-fun.

[33] John O'Donohue, *Beauty: The Invisible Embrace*, New York: Harper Perennial, 2005). https://www.goodreads.com/work/quotes/12339-divine-beauty-the-invisible-embrace accessed 6 JUL 2019.
[34] George Washington, *"George Washington to the New York Legislature, 1775*, http://www.loc.gov/teachers/classroommaterials/presentationsandactivities/presentations/timeline/amrev/contarmy/newyork.html accessed 29 JUL 2019. Punctuation has been modified for readability.